IN THE MODE OF DISAPPEARANCE

Winner of the 2006 Nightboat Poetry Prize

June 22, 2008 / Concord

To Edi—
It's been a true pleasure
to know you, and I
wish you all the best.
—Jonathan

IN THE MODE OF DISAPPEARANCE

POEMS BY JONATHAN WEINERT

Jonathan Weinert

NIGHTBOAT BOOKS   COLD SPRING, NY   2008

Nightboat Books
Cold Spring, NY

Library of Congress
Cataloging-in-Publication Data
Weinert, Jonathan, 1959 –
In the mode of disappearance / Jonathan Weinert.
   p. cm.
ISBN 978-0-9767185-7-4 (alk.paper)
I. Title.
PS3623.E43244515 2008
811'.6—dc22
2008008577

Original printing 2008
Design and typesetting: Jonathan Weinert

Cover painting: "Pacific" (1995), by Anne Stahl (www.annestahl.com). Oil, wax, and thread
on board. Used with the kind permission of the artist.

CONTENTS

S.

W.

ACKNOWLEDGMENTS

I am grateful to the editors of the following publications in which some of these poems first appeared, sometimes in slightly different versions:

American Letters & Commentary: "Variation on the Theme *I Am*"

Blood Lotus: "Narcissioné"

Blue Mesa Review: "Felipe Carillo Puerto" (section *v* of "To Xcalak")

Green Mountains Review: "New Earth"

Harvard Review: "Breakfast with Champion"

The Laurel Review: "Fair Affair of the Little 'I'"

LIT: "In the Mode of Disappearance"

The Louisville Review: "E-Mail in the Manner of Frank O'Hara," "A Night Out with Isabella de Hainaut"

Pleiades: "A Fiction"

Redactions: Poetry and Poetics: "Wellesley, Massachusetts," section *r*

32 Poems: "Sauve" (as "Le Village de Sauve")

Tuesday; An Art Project: "Solving for *y*"

"Manipura, Out of Tiphereth" appeared in *Cadence of Hooves: A Celebration of Horses*, ed. by Suzan Jantz (Yarroway Mountain Press, 2008).

Sincere gratitude to Brenda Hillman, for plucking my manuscript from the heap. Heartfelt thanks to all at Nightboat Books, particularly to Christina Davis for her careful reading, her ingenious editing, and her generosity of spirit. Christina, you're the bomb. Thanks to Allen Grossman and Joyce Peseroff for showing me the road, to Janet Sylvester for putting me on the road, and to Steven

Cramer for accompanying me on the first leg of the journey. Thanks also to Thomas Sayers Ellis, Molly Peacock, Debra Kang Dean, and Greg Pape for their guidance and inspiration while I was writing these poems. My deep appreciation to my son Noah, for being there and for making me proud. A bouquet of Fair Biancas to Leesteffy Jenkins for her encouragement and support, and for believing in me even when I believed in myself. For their friendship, and for reading and commenting on various incarnations of this book, a tip of the plume to Penny Dickerson, Marci Rae Johnson, Erin Keane, Diane Natale, Jae Newman, K. Alma Peterson, and Craig Williamson.

And, especially, to Amy M. Clark—all my love.

FOREWORD

Like is only *like* since the world was lost.
The world was lost twice. Once

when *is* fell out of *isn't yet*. Twice
when *is* fell into *is no more*.

Jonathan Weinert opens his collection with a spare "Song of Urthona," which plucks its playful but dire song on the strings lent to him by William Blake's cosmology. In Blake's poems, Urthona presides over the creative principle, and bears the impact both of the Kantian sublime as well as Milton's pre-lapsarian Eden into the Romantic era. Weinert's version of Urthona makes its own symbolic nature using delicate italics to set up contrasts between words and phrases, importuning creation to sort out its own powers. His Urthona does not eschew reason, has the capacity for making distinctions and for being a powerful figure to whom we might entrust redemptive care. Yet Weinert's italics-angel is also studious, bending over the homologies of "like" and "like"—noting the way likeness falls out of the world once you compare anything to anything. Channeling Spinoza polishing the lenses of creative reason, making language pass through time in order to reverse itself, the poet asserts, "*Isn't yet* is heaven. / *Is no more* is hell." I am admiring of this contemporary recasting of the Blakean force—seed-sorter, distinguisher of sensual impressions—that knows the world as Spinoza knows the silver brain of the clock and its avarice.

The formal intelligence of the collection is inspiringly complex, as is the moral and psychological engagement with the situations at hand. This moral complexity is expressed in personal and political dilemmas—both in fragmentary forms and in sweeping lyricism. The poet is careful with the heft of each word. "It's only the small / mortal sentence / that survives us, spoken by / my lips directly / in your oceanic ear," he writes in "E-Mail in the Manner of Frank O'Hara." The title itself, *In the Mode of Disappearance*, is a phrase that allows two nouns to engage the gears neither would have in isolation.

It is felicitous that the collection is being published by Nightboat, a ghost-vessel for poetry that calls up the varied traditions of modernisms and post-modernisms. Weinert's poems continually toggle between categories: there are echoes of Crane, Williams, Stevens, Stein as well as of contemporary heirs of those poets. The long title poem recasts iambic lines with meditative restraint. Weinert's subject matter is inclusive, and the best poems address the project of making consciousness in poetry, the title poem being Weinert's own "Notes Toward a Supreme Fiction" with a surrealist cast.

The poet employs diapason and smoke. He has reconciled himself to the haphazard nature of memory both rationally and irrationally. Individual poems sometimes use rhyme—both end-rhymes and embedded rhymes—yet reading the rhymed poems, I had the sensation that rhyming in this work is less about making sounds meet than it is about slicing across those meetings, calling up an internal violence—again, the figure of Urthona comes up—in ways that traverse diagonally across safe and true zones in order to locate themselves in the workings of experience.

The structure of the book nods to four traditional wind-sped directions, then spins out of them, creating secret elements; a poem in which Narcissus address-es his facelessness ("Narcissioné") is set next to a poem in which a dream-lake disappears then reappears in a Stevens-esque reader, calmly reading the lake back to its own surface ("A Fiction"). The poems about family seem both quasi-personal and reminiscent of the quandaries of the individual in any scene of the elaborate myth; the poet knows the captivated Platonic Caliban of the soul: "They say the soul's confined within a cave; / it fastens on a world of things and longs / to feather up again . . ." Weinert's "I" has biography and form and certain-ly gathers significance by being named in places—as a bird might have countless names in different languages, yet the life of "I" is realized by relinquishing its project; the poet Ivan Lalic tells of it thus (in Charles Simic's translation): "What I see I cannot describe; / I am its description." The poems are often beautifully abstract and specific, opening with each phrase—"I blazed   and burned   and fell // down / among the earth's exquisite arches . . ." It's a pleasure to introduce this subtle and lovely book.

BRENDA HILLMAN
California 2007

The cosmos . . . is in some way clearly touched by narcissism.
The world wants to see itself.

—GASTON BACHELARD

Reality is very nice as an idea, but who wants to look at it in
the face?

—CHARLES SIMIC

SONG OF URTHONA

Like is only *like* since the world was lost.
The world was lost twice. Once,

when *is* fell out of *isn't yet*. Twice,
when *is* fell into *is no more*.

Isn't yet is heaven.
Is no more is hell.

The thing that is will always be because
it was.

Some promises, once given,
cannot be taken back.

N.

NARCISSIONÉ

Driven—all this desperate green.
Headless (a man without a head).
An image in the window-sheen
(the left one). Another's life instead.

I found this *I* who saw the bright
ash living in the ash above
the Shawsheen strip mall. Damaged light.
One breath. What's *he* remember of

that time when—what? I loved? I learned?
I don't know *who* that is. He's here
in instances. He might return
and bring his solstice with him. Near

the lake that burned (the lovely one),
my house of sticks. No one who *knows*
me knows about that place. I've gone,
sometimes, mid-sentence. I'm so close

my face is faceless in the water.
Half in love. And half unwanted.

A FICTION

The lake was swallowed and it was
no longer lake. It started being
prohibited to pass a thing
and let that thing remain without

our sense of it abiding with
whatever it had now become.
The forests were replaced with other
forests, the lake with something like

a lake, but lacking water's taste
or how it darkens everything
it touches. Houses by the cove
were not the houses that were placed;

the lights that came on in the third
floor windows were the lights we caused
to flicker there; if they were home
they hadn't chosen to be nor

were they, in actuality,
themselves; the book he read was not
a written book; he wasn't moved
in an objective sense; the pain

she felt was not her pain, although
it stabbed her; though he had and had
not cheated on her; though he would
and would not cheat on her again.

The slow clock ticked and did not tick;
the housefly walking on his hand

was not about to land, nor was
he ever going to flick it off;

he could not feel nor realize
so long as we were looking in,
so long as we were making up
the fiction that was him to us,

by seeing him, by recognizing
what we saw. The total place
was not, nor could it ever be,
between us. We were as alone

as he, as indeterminate
despite its markings as the wren
we rendered on the lawn. He woke,
transfixed us with his gaze, and saw.

CRY

Last night I dreamed I was milling about a sort of food court
with people from a former job, jesting in that private language
only close associates enjoy. We were deciding what to have.
One woman held a two-volume desk reference
of psychological disturbances—she'd come from class,
and chatted with a half-bored colleague sporting trim Vandyke
and muttonchops. They seemed so self-possessed—so young
but so grown up, like those I knew before the complications.

In my pack, a thick book of poems with a Mark
Rothko cover, mostly black with lozenges of red,
the large white lettering knocked out—someone's *Collected*.
I thought I'd sit and read from it while everyone was deciding
so they all could see how sensitive I was; or, staring at the regular
half-moon pattern scored into the food court tiles, I thought
about a friend who'd died and what impression it would make
if I mentioned his death, weeping a little if I could manage it.

Just then I heard a cry—as of an animal or strangled child
—a scream choked off. I snapped awake and waited—
listening, not breathing, by the window.
                                    Late cars hushed
along the bottom of the hill, while farther off
a freight train spit and boasted as it slowed through town.

Then I heard my son moving in the kitchen, terrified
he might knock and ask, and what would I say to him,
while shadows barred and crossed the ground.

ARCANUM XXII: THE PINIONED MAN

A man sprawls face down in a paddock, pinned,
a long-sword through his back — *transfixed*, we say,
as if prostration were a thrust-in blade.
To miss the mark, the Bible says, is sin.

The postulant, it follows, must be nailed
to something other — earth or God or past
or mother . . . Yesterday, the last
imperfect rose still clinging to the failed

trellis of a neighbor seemed
the perfect metaphor for something I'd
prefer to disbelieve. That's why they lied
in Eden, I suspect: to be redeemed

from likeness so complete their blood would beat
against His blood or else not beat. In fact
the actor was contingent on the act.
The man lies, sliced with cold. A pointed sleet

obliterates the field, where nothing grows.
His paradise is nothing that he knows.

NEW EARTH

I fled from heaven's ordinance.

There was a field of gentians there
patched with lilies —
lily-faces white with expectation.

On earth, the sun was setting for the final time.

Everything was passing out of sight,
like shadows blown apart by wind.

Beyond the farthest plinth of cloud
a quadrant opened under me.

I saw the houses
patient by their pale lights,
shouldered underneath two hills.

I couldn't bear to chalk the lintels,
passing over each with heavy wings,

sparing them, for pity's sake,
who slept, suspecting nothing.

They woke and gathered in the square,
a strange light coming over them,

their lily-faces looking up,
expecting morning.

TUNNEL EGRESS TE-212

Everyone
    has one of me. Jumpsuit.
    Timberlands. A helmet
(winged). I bring the news. I

climb.
    Below, unlighted workers. Soles
    above. Defended people pausing
on the outskirts of their feet,

suspecting
    nothing. Suspect no
    populated darkness.
Below, my engines cough and crush,

sustaining.
    Roses in the shitpile. Each
    a port. Shades cache the eyeholes
even on Olympus. Even in this skanky

sunlight.
    Projection of the true world
    (nothing) on the platform (space),
but shoddy. The "causal world" is

all effect.
    Some will tremor with my head
    against the door (the undefended).
Some will never let me out.

Some
    will pry my eyes to see.
    Will know no terror of the darkness.
Slant in terror of the light. Some will.

ASIDE

It could have been the stand
of yellow willows by the river.
It could have been the single grackle
cracking seeds.

It could have been the silence
sleeping in the throats
of every man and woman in Ballardvale.
It could have been the iron of false dawn,
my kneeling on the pebbles on
the path beside the dam.

I prayed for weather as
the stones pressed
letters in my knees.

I raised my voice
against the cold, whose ghost went up
like swallowed signal smoke.

There ought to be a word
(it isn't death)
for the sudden yielding of one's fibers,
for the body's disengagement
and the silence after.

UNPLEASANT PARABLE OF THE SOUL

They say the soul's been chained within a cave;
it fastens on a world of things and longs
to feather up again . . .
                          I wouldn't know:
I crave confinements, deaf and dumb to all
such buzzings from above, compelled to keep
rehearsing my confession every time
some stranger blunders in.
                          But neither I
nor gin can stop her picking in my ribs,
licking the coal dust from her fingers, hard
about the business of her memory,
announcing what still has to be announced.

If there were a sweater with a self in it
if there were a sweater
with a cliff
if there were a sweater with the sun in it
at the 72nd parallel
that would be the thing   that would be
a glacier calving in the sea (blue like no one
blue like me) so

what then was I saying   self
with sweater at one bend of the universe
no more but ranges, ranges with a few
left outposts and
a few still cabins scattered in the hills
I'll give you
that   I'll give you   well
I'll give you nothing   but the thing

I am

is something, something neither here
something like
something (like nothing then   but
no not

even   Question (bruited gingerly): is you is?
the bones that bare
your face up sing the spangled quanta,
change, absorb the strangeness, evoke a field of force
with lines emerging
as the lines

emerge   oh you can't say it plainly in
2004   not that there aren't

still slack places
between the stations   not that there aren't
still whole midwests
of oblivion   not that there aren't still
gutters flush with their own
nostalgia   not
that there aren't   but

thingness and I-ness keep hatching it out
keep breathing and breaking and making
that noise like
antlers scraping up the shinbones
of a tree   like anthems
hemmed by nasal voices
in a minor key   but

isness and I-ness keep scratching it out
keep writing long   keep fantasizing
and underinhaling
like a god/balloon
like breathing   like the life I is and is
is like

the you that is or might be isn't
nt nt   the sick sick sound of iron riving bone
of ivy rising on the stone

Facing the weather is the last
refuge of the dying man   maybe that's
all you do   maybe that's
all you say   as the barked
astringent bendlight breaks
and makes its shinglefall

in varied boats

maybe you just know and is and am
without contingency   without the tangled
attributes   without

the getting and the making   maybe I is
place   a sweater with
or sans a self   and the lean long legs
of the last lorn light
highly striding
in the manufactured streets (your streets
the streets

you said you loved) and down the walls of
any houses   where all is
(isness
follows isness) you is I is
is   until such time

E.

WELLESLEY, MASSACHUSETTS

42°18'N, 71°17'W

a.

Returning after generations of myself

Between my street and the field
I flew my kite in, an ancient
                              alphabet of trees

(aspen, basswood, cherry,
dogwood, elm)
                    disgorging shadows
                    much the same
                    as in 1968

Unseasonably cool again
this summer day

Returning to myself
after generations of myself

b.

My family's grayfelt flannelled urban shadow
        out of Bucharest or Prague, Göttingen
        or Göteborg, Riga or Tallinn

        fell   across the lawns, the tennis courts,
        the fields, the manicured
                    estates —

the shadow of a blue-veined hand, slender,
large-knuckled, battered, stained
with India ink and crook'd
    with palsy, shaking ancestral hand
    palm downward

over all the clockfaced steeples, post fences
down on Grove along the hockey pitch,
Nehoiden's eighteen holes, the ivied college
library

c.

I walked and walked,
habitually alone along the brief
jaw of Eliot Street

> My double streamed behind me
> or before me long
> and slender like the finger
> of a boy

past the classroom building and the kite-flying field
hunched in the odor of money
hunched in the pale imperfect light
of Christian Science

> the hour silent as a toppled bell   its silver
> clapper lapsing out

d.

The shadow of a hand, a fist

A fist of words, oppression
        of the last how many centuries
        turned to milk and breath I fed on

Turned to breath and seed

and generation

e.

Broken lineage
out of old Romania
Hemlock-shadowed in the deep
hilled glades

Iosef urged two goats on ropes
along the only street before
the Sabbath in
his coat of many pieces

Soon the dark of wolves
and torches
sphering out

I picture this
from all the nothing
that was left
of it

Unsurnamed grandpa steamered
with a twist of money
sewn into a leathern
purse

with half a set of teeth in his head
How his left eye must have gleamed
in Ellis Island arclights
where the stories start

Make a name for us
grandpa

some old German thing
always west of where you were

Spend your gettings for us
never tell

that story

The one in which we find out
who we are

and where the darkness comes from

f.
I blazed   and burned   and fell

down
       among the earth's exquisite arches

(which meant)

Lamplight-reading in my feetsie pajamas
Liberal assassinations 1964
Tauntings at the school because my eyes
were changed

to shells or pearls

I should have had a say
I should have had
           a hand

g.

She couldn't know (this was my mother)
what spark was housed inside my chest-hill

A door with golden handle and a shadow
deep inside

Old man's shadow   Old man's eyes directing distant gleamings
on the back sides of my eyes   Beyond him there was

Nothing
Bliss of nothing . . .

Mother (absent) I call to you along the distances
You went to other countries how could I

have followed or maybe I had visas
the authorities denied you and you knew

I was your flesh but not your spirit
stretched beyond your limits

which were hills and cabins in a weepy valley
we stayed in for a week one summer

as the brochures lied

h.

4 p.m.   maypole / blue on streamer blue
                              forking out and out

Axis where the kite string led my eye
to disappearances
                    A white sky torched
                    with vapor-trails

Wind I could imagine up there scrubbed
away
            Sinews, calves / My deltoids working
            as I wound the string

Such tenderness

such léger
demain

i.

My grandma socked me in the eye.
My eye swelled up and closed.
I never had its use again this mortal life.

  My buried eye ranges in a narrow cleft.
  Sees the flesh and its obsequious lacquers.
  How it's made so straitly to obey.

I was nine or ten, I didn't do.
My mother must have been the same as me.
My grandpa selling on the road.

  I'm an evangelist of pain.
  I show my own son how to make it hurt.
  Woman is to tragedy as man

to absence. What could I have done?
My grandma showed me spaceships in the kiting trees.
Later, when her husband and her mind were gone.

  I show my son how to jeopardize trust.
  The pleasure in derision. How to wound
  his own good eye. To show he's one of us.

j.

Such anger borne
on such a blameless head

           (except the blame
           of generations

—on such a tender head
such appetites

k.
I'm in red, about to graduate
from H.S. 1977 June—

kite-flying fields behind me,
roasted white in sunlight.

I'm standing *contrapposto*, head
a little tilted to the left, straw-
colored center-parted hair to shoulders.

My right hand, awkward,
wrings the left,

my face is vague and sand-erased.

I look like every woman
I had ever lost, or would.

1.

My mother stuck a scrannel reed
into "the porches of mine ears"
and sluiced the hollow instrument
down the stairway of my throat

I couldn't after speak and then
through that inserted straw her bee-
mouth sipped some sweetness from my gut.
"Just let, just let"—again again

she stuck the reed—I let her—let
my substance be the stuff of her
and that was love, or love's demand—
my love of her that way. In time

we let the caudex stand, and root,
for ease, despite the pain, and fixed
two sucked-out grackle's eggs on each
already sparkless eye, like Themis—

feminine and blind. I was for use,
a ventriloquial device
—the bellows for another's breath,
the plexus for another's need.

—"What hidden lord and master, and cruel,
remorseless emperor commands me?"
—"It had been good for that man, if
he had not been born." So many voices,

I couldn't after hear the one
almost inaudible assertion,

blood beneath the shushing of
the blood, the uninhabited,

immortal tone.

m.
One Sunday dawn

closed shop mouths along Central,
the Congregational still as any noonday,
headstone-still (the quiet Congregationalists
buttoned in the collar of their faith)—

No trains below the Weston bridge, no cars
the whole way down to Town Line Liquors
nor the other way to Dover and the farm-stands—
My best friend Dave sleeping in his low-roofed house

(17something)—dragonflies sleeping
in the marsh behind the swimming beach at Morse's Pond—
My parents sleeping, and my sister, and
my baby brother, and Fran the cat—A pure

light over everything, the light of Torah
(*b'reisheet*) or the blessèd end—

My father's office sign (Frank Weinert
=Optometrist) creaked a little
in a lifting breeze, all of Wellesley Square
a little creaked—

like a trap door slowly rising then to close
on me with one foot on the cellar stairs,
the dream on narrow jointed legs coming up
to meet me

n.

I walked and walked   the dark
maple line eating at the sky
behind Wellesley College

of the spire

of the garden

1975   Dave and I ate green glass bottles
on the bridge we called the Arches by
the golf course and the Charles

We ate them as we ate the nights
all summer—dry grass, dope, the talk
all night of stars and records

A hundred years ago the carriage roads
conveyed the Hunnewells
through unburned woods
beyond the shiftings
of the bees they kept

o.

The road where Simon lived went up
      and doglegged left
      to aspen stands
      The hill primeval

      with the absence of its houses

Lights along the bottom of the hill

                        went out before the sun

                        It was the first day of everything
                        and I a sort of Adam hid

                        ashamed of my nakedness
                        and the world's

                        I lanced my side
                        and dipped the sponge in vinegar

                        to clean the wound of vision

All these years the wound
still stings
      No stone for me
      No three days' absence

p.

1967   I played with Mark who lived next door
His mom would make us lunch
and I could hardly understand

        such gentility
        in chicken salad sandwiches

        waiting always
        for the blow to fall

1974   Dave and I
would steal his brother's Tofranil
and zone out after school

Simon with a brace of toughs
confronted us on Cameron
in front of Hunnewell

We were cowards
but we called ourselves "non-violent"

while they

took whatever bothered them
out by taunting us—

Harmless, until Simon breathed
You fucking kike
You had it coming

q.

Down then

             from the raised position
                   Down the sledding-hill
                   until the kite-flying field

We bite snow from clipped-on mittens
My sister hauls ahead of me
rising up to where

we enter cycle once again
Potential spent in falling via track
                   where end is seen
                   but still unknown

Looking up through stripped branches of the kiting-trees
New England stormfront 1963 promising a further snow
Sky a dirty undershirt with the boy's
still-beating heart unstill inside it
to be thumped and cleaned

r.

Behind the stables

sixteen horses stabled out
behind Tenacre

In conference with the principal
one morning (March)   I was four
and mom was there

Conscious of some nonexistent wrong
I took solace in
the Russian dolls
one inside another

seeking for the smallest
most interior one

who couldn't be divided

s.

We walked and walked   (this was Dave and I)

the back   one hundred acres
let fallow by the college

Pines along the lips of hollows
Basins full of sand
Aspen, stands of alder—
oak

Stripped in winter but the pines
were green

Freeze-foot   foot-foot   snow-foot
boot-foot
                tree-foot   Dave-foot
                        I-foot

under arches   with the drug inside

                        until the cytoplasm
                        in our foot-cells
                        froze
                        We were happy

                        having met the hemlock
                        on its terms

                        having been the hemlock

Solar plexus
                and the divagating tree
                were joined

t.

Snow-boots   crusted snow   the whorl
where plowblades scarred the ice

                       with grit
                       beside the power station

                       where the unmapped land began

It wasn't Greenland
               but it was
             inside

u.

I dreamed, I watched the body breathe. Which I
    was I? I studied letters in a thick
        grimoire. I dreamed, I watched the body breathe.

I walked along a narrow ditch, red wheat
    grew higher than my eyes. I dreamed I watched
        the body breathe. I learned to levitate

beneath a castle's groined arcade. I dreamed,
    I watched. The body breathed. *Knock-knock* I woke,
        or fell into that other dream,

which realer seemed. I walked
    to school; I did whatever children do.
        The schoolyard drifted light, and burned.

v.

After twentyone days

                         sick in bed

                         as March occurred

one Sunday after snow

before the new growth blurred the tamarack

I walked out across the kite-flying field

                         listing from the bed

                         I'd dreamed in

Was I sick   (I don't recall)

I could have faked it

This was real: if I closed my eyes

                         my indignation might

                         invent a voice

when I emerged   and I would be

at last   an other

Maybe god had made mistakes   the world

                         some perfect nonappearing thing

                         he shattered

into evidence   because he couldn't wait

or maybe he was careless   and I've tried forever since

to gather all its pieces   I walked across the kite-flying field

                         Blunt chisels of the sun

                         were chipping eskers

in the drifts   a map of quadrants

cold and far   I stepped in one step over ranges

blue half-frozen   whitecapped bays
                and then the Pole
                unpeopled
slightly west of where   the compass told
The last place ever   or the first

w.

They poisoned the Charles
so thoroughly its stench
would force our windows up
whenever we'd drive along it
to the highway
and the sea

A tributary sluiced through backlots
down behind the houses
off of Livingston

green and slow and flaked
with islands

     Charles lay down
     His head a crown of tangles
     where the mallards drowsed

     I oared that way
     one late in August afternoon
     along his long blood

     Shinbones carving banks
     His tarsals where the current baffled out
     in spreads and channels

     Bee sounds simmered in the brakes
     Hornbeam hung precisely over stream
     The redness dozing in its leaves

     He turned his face a little south and breathed
     sleeping for the coming wished-for change
     his fingers laced across his breastplate

x.

What were those structures   holding great
        cut stones aloft   above an absence

        Looking up   at any hour
I tried to guess   the moment when

the keystone   mortarless
        would loosen like a tongue   and lapse—

        a blow more crushing   since it never fell
How many times   did I petition the geometry

of stone dismantling bone   the brain's bright impulse
        sparking for a moment   in the dusk

        then nothing to obstruct   the bitter flavors
rising from the spines   of burnt-out cattails

in the river's mouth   silence
        falling on the 18th green   like a solved equation

        They were there   in rich flesh
in the first part   of the evening

We called them Mom and Dad   although their names
        were Jachin, Boaz   Aye

        and Naught   Bitter Salt and Bitter Fire
They moved apart   on either section

of the sectioned couch   smiling for nothing
        before the butcher's eldest daughter came   to handle us

Whatever they desired   they didn't say
I didn't know there was   desire

except my own   to crush
          or be allayed   There was nothing

          between them   and above them
great weight hung   and held

y.
Beneath the apple tree that only gave us
    small apologetic apples

my father grilled. *His* father held forth, in his kept
    Moldavian accent. His origins unknown,
    he took the country's birthday as his own.

The women of the last two generations
    (coats on, purses clutched despite July)

ranged a dozen lawn chairs in an arc
    and spoke all afternoon
    the foreign female tongue.

            Something high was loosed among the trees:
            a sibilance indistinct but desperate to be heard

            It drove me to the kite-flying field to crouch
            beneath the arches of the oaks

            while far off laughter swept in tatters
            through the dropping breeze —

            The interrupted whine
            of thirteen-year cicadas hoisted up

            a yellow flag against the sky, which turned
            all afternoon about a vanishing

        At dusk the sky's flag fell   across the severed lawns and leaves
        and limber water odors   rose
        to build a shadow in the sky   that drained all color

The relatives lingered, murmuring in clusters
     over yellow cake and tea,

until the last red tail-light shifted
     down the half-lit strait of Eliot
     to be swallowed at the turn.

z.

Unseasonably cool   June 10th
      I set one foot   and then another
         on the trail

         the mountains Green and White ahead of me

     I sent some packets in advance
     to certain P.O.'s on the route —

         Shelburne / Conway / Monson:

     food for living off the grid,
         gauze for wounds,
         a set of trail-guides bound in drab,

         maps to show me where I will have been

     and better still, what wasn't sent:
         the evenings falling on the sprinklered lawns
         without my help . . .

One deep post-noon
         coming down the steep east slope
         of Moosilauke

         my pack-frame caught up on a wire
         slung between two ash

         to favor the ascent
         of south- and westbound hikers

Hanging there   my feet were feet above the ground

and I could neither walk nor fall

hoisted on my burden

A few leaves dropped among the stones and ferns
The pattern of the shadows changed
Countless microscopic things were lifted in the light and ceased

My body somehow struggled free of that
and found the blaze ahead

S.

BOARDED — 42° 15′ N., 60° 35′ W.

You back in, first with praise and then
with piracy. Sword of tongue, your left eye
glinting like the sea's, which rakes

and buries. Crewless I defend, your pinnace
fast against my bulwarks. There's the hogshead
crammed with diamonds, there's the spice

of Araby, there's the gilt mask of the dead
Moroccan king. They're yours before I know it.
I've got sticks and stocks and stubborn sheets,

a poise of mainsail, jib, a certain angle
to the wind. You say nothing but it's wrong,
you'll change it soon, that heading. Then will I

unwheel below decks where it's cramped and dark.
Those vacant quadrants on the chart are only sweet
if unassailed. Of course the mess of ropes

and chains, of course the reeking galley,
of course the corpses in the second hold.
You find them out, you log them, I was fool

and bilge-drunk flagrag when I thought of hiding.
Soon you're in the sherry casks, the caskets
flush with gold doubloons, the brown rhine stuffed

behind the bulkheads — all my treasures,
and the black pearls of the slave restraints
glowering in the halflight. The jig is up. You raise

and cure your cutlass edge to stripe me
as I gutter and release, colorless to ward you,
complaisant, then, defending nothing.

MANIPURA, OUT OF TIPHERETH

This fierce horse stumbles from my stable-plexus—
sixteen hands, star both fetlocks, sorrel coat,
no vices, tends to pace when nervous:
        caveat rider.

Earthcurve's grave and gravity, her cure
for yellow cantering. Fever-fled,
she's paddocked in the middle orchard
        facing east and ocean.

Chew that. She craters January pasture,
green shoots creeping under: succulents
and paralytics. A bridle ruse
        can check her.

Her dam's a famous champion, named
for beauty—She's got her eyelights, heat,
and tremor. Smooth her to the sea-fed sky,
        the vital nova.

You'll find she's tried, goes nicely driving double,
foot-clod, clad and roan, her bloodclash spurred
or coaxed with sugar. Keeps her head. Carries
        whom she will.

FAIR AFFAIR OF THE LITTLE "I"

Kissed me, little rocket.
                    Up, our backs
against the fulcrum. Over everything,
some scrim of golden dust. You changed me
but you didn't want to talk about it.
                        Down,
tethered to the center. All those other couples
—glossies from a notice. How they did it.

Still, you wanted me.
                Altocumuli
licked crystals from our lips, spun them ·
into sugar, waxed prolific, fled, then
spilled them in the sea, whose spume went sweet.
Could almost see it from the zenith.

Our vision of the river blocked
by many trees.
              Some revolutions
you would leave your body's silver housing,
drawn aloft by aches you couldn't help
reliving. I held your envelope
until you climbed back in it. Shifted all
your vision to your male right eye. Saw shapes
I couldn't see.
             Along the fencing
by the Ferris wheel
(to keep the riffraff out) October
pressed its clear advantage. Weather everywhere
was all about me.
              Then I couldn't breathe.

MOON

Bone of my bone

White sliver of my eye

Print of my little finger

Thin white honey on the ground

What shapes of you are moved about the woods

Chess with only ivory kings

To slay each other in the black

Shadows you inscribe

Between the frosted pines

And all the old legitimate armies

Bearing off in lines

To vanish in the hustings of the reeds

And there you are again

Looking up from water

Cake of ice

Or soap

IN THE MODE OF DISAPPEARANCE

1.

What good's the world if it can't be lived from
the last cabana of the human and
its notebook, blank but promising so much
because its promise isn't given. Soon
the shade that opens in your breathing lets
and lets, it isn't kindness, surely, but
a kind of conversation between your voice
and the absence of a voice. Effacement's not
a novelty but everything adjacent
to it seems renewed. One wants to be
a frame for someone else's image, harmless
as a space which isn't harmless since
it's stuffed with content, canvas and the stiff
stacked strokes and colors, surfaces and then
more surfaces. The picture's not as nuanced
as it's meant to be, but inside's fiction,
or a coast retreating as description
keeps approaching it, the rumor of
a golden country which, when overrun,
projects one in the posture of conquistador.

2.

You want to see the coast before the feast,
to spend an uninflected hour or two
but even that's accounted for, as is
the liminal town, its little figures prim
with habit, sleeves and windy hats without
intention, digging ditches, sipping coffee,
dripping in the screenhouse of emotions where
the harbormaster's dogs are hanging out.
You dared to live among the model palms
and now they're real within your definitions
of the real. But in the mode of disappearance
you fall out of things exactly in proportion
to your understanding, such that understanding
everything ensures your total disappearance
from the world of things, and from the memories
of things, which will forget you; you are not
the subject of the pre-sorbet discussion
while the white gloves go on signing in the air,
the courses are removed which didn't harm
the appetite, and all your dust is huddled
end to end to make a long uncommon
body recognized no more as body
but as landscape or as lateness of the hour.

3.

Suppose you want an absence, as you do.
It isn't fatal but it's dangerous,
it's taxing for your neighbors building lean-tos
on the marshy fringes of your tendency
to have so many selves, each one a point
that you keep making in both argument
and space, distorting the continuum
exactly as the theory predicated.
You want, and want, and there it is, you need,
and that engenders turbulence perceived
as thing: a hurricane inside a house.
The weather changes, but it is; along
the sound a lexicon of uncoined words,
a payroll whose accounts are overdue.
Suppose you close the screenhouse windows, still
you're less concerned with what to say than how
to say it, as it isn't written in
the manifest, whose products pink the sea.

4.

It isn't going to be like that, not
any more, as the sun of thinking that's
expressed its strangeness like a blond desire
for darkness, which is how the quasars blink
the tears of their departing back, or so
the schismatists of tears attest, who don't
in any case agree. It has to do
with you because, in changing, Who-You-Were
continues swinging in its track, a vair
planet with many foci, or an eye
that keeps consuming its fifteen acetates
in a predetermined sequence. On the street,
for instance, something happened between you
and someone and it made you feel some way,
it's still important since it's happening now,
you can keep going back to it to check
its premises and colors, or to change
a troubling detail, which you're technically
allowed to do. The allegations lodged
against you stick to you like sunlight, violet
on the head and copper in the face. You go
on past the hope of pardon, mattering.

5.

It's tolerable if it's the last one but
it's not, its series is the wing of some
enormous house against which light that used
to be effective batters feebly,
deflects one quantum at a time without
illumination, while the bells of many
convents waver whitely in the air.
They're almost shoeless in their vanity
but you have densities to opalesce,
whole chapters which a mouth invents. You aren't
relieved, not yet, although the downstairs beds
have all been slept in and the upstairs maids
have fled. You know it's you whose shape each pillow
favors, every gesture is a room,
each variation of the head, each trick
articulation, like a prism barred
with bands of red. You raise the spoon, you raise
the spoon, you raise the spoon, you eat, you eat,
you eat, you touch a finger to your face
and that repeats with other latencies,
each one of them, continuous at last,
until your fiction figures every sheet.

6.

If violet is the color of a moored
condition, copper is the color of
that mooring doubtfully reflected, changed
the way a habit changes, slowly and
without the tidy sound of bells, but then
the fluctuating elsewhere is itself
a sort of habit, one you can't control
or else don't want to, having sacrificed
one color for another, and your voice
becomes a category of some other
voice addressing parties who are not
the same ones as before. You predicate
"Carnation Redefined as Rose," or "Un-
disputed Area," until your ghost
instantiates a shadow underneath
some date palms ranged along a shore you don't
exactly recognize but which feels like
home: Long dark knife, the handle of a bone,
a stick of markings from the first antique
remembrance, fire without its root in form.
If violet is the color of a bruise

7.

that keeps recurring elsewhere, copper is
the color of the bruising signature,
the instigation of a loop about
the blameless neck. It ought to be enough
to say the birches almost disappear
by virtue of a parody of sky,
black there against another photograph
of black, that sleep is continuity's
approach to certain questions one is not
prepared to ask. It ought to be enough
to say what one has always meant to say.
If this is execution then the artist
hasn't stayed within the lines. You're like
a third wife barely in the family frame,
effaced but not effaced enough, you have
whole sequences of colors yet to un-
dergo, whole sentences to carry out.
What good's the world if it can't be lived from?
It ought to be enough to say the ships
beyond that line of trees are satisfied
to strain against their moorings, even though
the undertow compels them in that line.

8.

The broken one remembers everything,
whatever's in the frame or was in frame,
as though an afterimage were the next
incursion of a person or a thing,
assuming properties for which you can't
conveniently account. You have the sense
that nothing's happened even once and won't
be happening again, at least not soon,
but there's the whole extent of it: it is,
the way a tropical depression is
when seen from satellite remove, and then
you're right down in it and the aftermath,
occurring simultaneously, becomes
a candidate effect, although it could
be cause. The little figures living through it
scrape their deck chairs on the dock and watch
the permutations of the sea, which should
be calm of ships and disappearances,
a Caribbean diffidence but neutral,
battery with two plus terminals,
but then it's not. The colors won't relax
or loose their oils in logical succession:

9.

It's all at once, or else it's not at all.
The broken one remembers everything
because it happens at a distance. Soon
the gloved attendants haul the last cabanas
up the shore, well clear of those encroachments
made and remade in the sea's account
of lapses, which one reads as bulletins
or other latest figments of the news.
The sky, dyed dark then darker than a ruse,
suggests a denouement too cavalier
to credit. To the left and slightly north
the conversations drift among the palms
like little storm fronts swinging out to sea,
and in the space their absence makes one sees
the golden country as the unobserved,
both post and prior to its history,
unmade but total as a thing all done,
a place you want to visit, live in, but
you know that simply looking at destroys.
The notebook, there but not yet written in,
provides the best, most accurate account,
as readers of the series will affirm.

W.

THOMAS BALL CONFRONTS THE FUTURE

A hump of broken body parts, all bronzed—
a hoof adjacent to the great man's eye,
two fingers crushed beneath a chunk of mane,

the flaring nostrils pressed against the fine
high foreleg, and the cornered hat dislodged
to rest upturned atop the pedestal

in Boston's Public Garden, in the rain.
Nearby, the high Prudential offices
stood idle, slack. The beacon of the old

John Hancock, shattered in St. James, made cribs
for scavengers and derelicts. No birds
were camping in the new-growth trees, which sapped

and branched and panicled despite the lack
of any human husbandry. White cones
of flowerets plunged before a green the wind

blew up into an agitated sea
projected on the lower sky's dull scrim,
a pink light pouring from its littoral.

A dim pink light kept pouring in the sky
above the absent hat of Washington,
the broken seats, the tulip beds, the plaques

that named them grown into the flesh of rare
imported trees. Destruction made the world
the world's museum.

The Father of Our Country and his horse
lay broken, slumped together on the path.
The light kept pouring from its final source.

AIR ROUTES OF THE WORLD (DAY)

Ben Langlands & Nikki Bell, screenprint 2001
Speed Art Museum, Louisville

I wonder what that northbound flight
is all about: parabola
whose fin-like silhouette describes
a foiled escape, as if the Pole

were limit—not the limit of
a surface, not the limit of
dimension, not the limit of
velocity, but the limit of

one's tolerance for tension. First
the path sweeps up from Paris, points
above the Arctic, then deflects
acutely for New York. One flight

originates in Bogotá,
I think, then magpies west to—where?
some island paradise? And what
about that arrow pronging east

beyond what ought to be Tierra
del Fuego? The stretched net of routes
suggests the absent continents,
their shapes still visible behind

its mesh of unnamed knots, the way
a lover's body might hump up
beneath a coverlet, asleep.
It makes a constellation of

our settlements, a pattern of
some vague yet mythical portent,
as if it could explain to us
the disappearance of our cities,

or show us where the hell we're going
and why we keep returning there,
and what could happen in between
the destinations, in the blanks.

TO XCALAK

i. Merida

Far from the sea the morning red
Shops along the main
drag shut and all the locals
in the street—

each shop a model of
the total world   all colors
blare through mirrors
of the storefront glass

The street the surface
of a brilliant sun
above which two embracing figures
tremble in the heat

Roots emerge from joints
of concrete stairs
beneath a piñon pine
at one end of the broken block

Sky rising
over all of it

ii. Cobá

New pavements sealing in
old stones   the stones asleep

Two thin bitches watching shadows
inching toward the absence of
whatever happens next

iii. Tulum
Stink of cheap cigars
Unbuilt pavements
façades   *mercados*

Cubans under glass—

A people can be sold
but no one's buying

Stink of cheap guitars
the new Convenience

Gates and armed attendants
at the entrance to the pool

The greens at Playacar
poisoning the coming
and receding sea

iv. Limones
That is no place but someone
lives there

Our headlamps flash
against the fuel pump

at the turn

Cosmos of a room
a schoolchild sleeps in

He knows the story
but has never been
to Yaxchilan or Calakmul

The story is a wheel of no color
touching the horizon
every way

   v. Felipe Carillo Puerto
Blare of trumpets from a box

Old man with broken shoes
selling blankets in a filthy linen suit
the color of a dried-out section
of a honeycomb

Close rooms in walls
the color of an aqua sea
above a bank

Smells of sweat and honey
and the taste
of dust on stucco

Before the town a paper shack
in scrub
and then the town
and then beyond the town
a paper shack in scrub

Its roof blew off in last night's rain
but the living there have nothing

so they build another shack
a quarter mile away

At night the darkness is a sea
they've all drowned beneath

The lights are far enough away
they look like rescue ships
a Coke machine beside the drugstore
in Limones
foundering

and on the surface of the sea
each morning
hundreds of lethargic bees

vi. Calakmul
Partway up the limestone plain
miles of uncut forest

Ramón trees shoulder up
among the stones

to hide them

Plaits of braided hair were laid
on balustrades beside the rough
steps up the east face of the platform

as an offering

They disappeared not far from there
They filled the temples in the city square
with rubble and the animals returned
by virtue of whose spirits they could move
to other entrances
between Canopus and The Swan

They used the jackal and macaw
The small cut jaguars cried from every wall
of the dreaming chambers

   vii. Xcalak
Before the last
line of breakers
on Chinchorro's edge

a mile offshore   no ships
the slates outside our sliding doors
obscured by drifts

Braided ropes belay the streets
for taking time   We slow the car
to see each roadside leaf—

both drab and silver sides
and how each branch grows out
among them into space

without instruction   The school looks new
but everyone is fishing
We drink tequila on the beach

The sun is putting out its fires
behind us as the wind comes up
Then night

The stars' lamped windows poise
an inverse city high
above the black

unpopulated sea

SAUVE

If I could climb into death now
as into a foreign car, where
in all of France would you drive me?

The sun all day and all last week
has set just south of the cathedral
on a rise one town away.

It's afternoon here, even in the mornings,
when the sun gets up and rolls
along its edge. The trees immediately below
its circuit burn, but then the next day
there they are, all green again.

If death is not a car he still may come,
rich man too thin for August,
with hairs in either ear
and apologetic beard, forgetting
what we put him on the earth for.

He was the one, at last, who couldn't bear
the sunlight on the stones
for very long. He was the one
who couldn't stand that matter
promised paradise,
that substance was the one

unbroken promise, while
the dented shingles of the Rieu-Massel
still slid below the bridges.

ST-BRESSON

Sun-gold on the southwest wall
stripped in the last millennium
to show the first stones
poised together—filings underneath
a magnet passing over.

Honey, gold, and amber:
perfect pitch and spit and excrement,

unconscious as the hills above Roquedur
at our velocity, a slow
concatenation blindly made,
like us,
of other lives.

It isn't plaster that preserves us
—not the beams and not the roofs
of snapped red tile.

Insect life is sticky,
all those veined transparent wings
that catch the sunlight striking up
the valley with the river
and its name.

This is how the disappearance
knits its covering:
one membrane at a time.

E-MAIL IN THE MANNER OF FRANK O'HARA

1.

And anyway my train was late, we waited
twenty-five minutes in the rain which was long
and ropy as an acrobat's veins
      Yes!   Delete those two messages, they sound
      nefarious and referred, like Donatella's
                      illnesses

    How do they find us in this world
        who planned on meeting
        only on the bridges!
    We have numbers addresses
        patterns of charges on
        magnetic disks
    which signify, like everything,
        nothing   It's only the small
        mortal sentence
    that survives us, spoken by
        my lips directly
        in your oceanic ear
    without the intervening cables

2.

When it rains it's like South Station is
at one end of the rue de l'Odéon
and at the other end that elm I saw you walking under
You were wearing a black wool coat down to your ankles

You looked well but you wouldn't speak to me
I guessed your silence was the darling hat
you'd purchased at Les Halles, with the three
red berries on a fine black mesh

Two of them are poisonous, the third
one makes you see

BREAKFAST WITH CHAMPION

Adonis breaks the handle from your cup,
says *Here*. That was your favorite cup.
No good telling yourself that any old cup
would just as nicely do. You want no cup
but that one: plain blue glaze, handmade, a cup
that no one else would covet, lopsided, cup
in concept if not a perfect cup in execution.
And he's so handsome—not a blemish on him.
And you're so flattered that he condescends
to talk with you, flounced up on the kitchen chair
in your three-days-worn-together bathrobe,
hair a nest, no makeup, not one concession
to the discipline of seeming, nothing
propping you up, while he's all golden
with his cornflower eyes like suction cups,
his body like a fist of art. He makes the other cups
invisible.
          But suddenly you're tired
of him, his standard shine. You want the lax
gut, the lanky hair, the listing and the thick lip
where the potter screwed the perfect motion
of his wheel. You're screwed like that. That's why
they made a place for you on earth. That's why
you never cry at funerals. That's why
you're wide awake, you're blued.

A NIGHT OUT WITH ISABELLA DE HAINAUT

Semper eadem: 1184–2004

Your arm, your right arm, hairless, honeyed,
with the velvet sleeve pushed halfway up
between the elbow and the ulnar carpal
is the queen of France's. Your hand closes
on a flute of port, its finger with the ring
of mercy pointing toward a resolution
for the warring factions—Normandy
and Flanders. In your sleep last night you chewed
the smallest finger of your right hand's nail
remembering Artois, imagining
the crown of your dominion lifted up
in a cloud-winged hand, as on the Ace of Cups,

which signals unity and love of strength.
In the middle distance, the Dominican
barback approaches with his filthy rag,
clears our two drained glasses, asks us—pale,
apologetic—if we want another.
Prayerfully, he smooths his belted uniform,
bowing to something untranslatable.
Outside, a coast of pigeons angles from
the plaza empty as the ocean off
Pointe de Barfleur that night you were smuggled in
from Weymouth. Cold streets, Bay Village, the slippage
of time and space which signals an incursion.

Your bright encampment swallows the whole city.
Passing between the tents, I watch your thighs,
their regnant contours working in a slip
of light black fabric. Now I think I know
what queens are for, what rule and measure mean.
Soon, when we kiss, black standards rasp against

strapped linden saplings, elms, a fleur-de-lis
of lamplight striping shadow grates across
two yards. I close my eyes so I can see
you (taste of white lily, vanilla, leaf).
You bend a little from your regency
and move among your troops, according courage.

THE HAIR CONCERTO

I. Allegro

So much the windlass, as I've come to think
your hair is, less and less the differences
between the two directions of the sky,
which seeks to drift as all appearances
inscribed in this addendum tend to do
—accounts of kidnap and of near escape,
although the latter don't convince, as none
has come this way since winter spread its sheet
among the birches propped along the fence,
lifelike but without the staginess
of life, which one suspects is elsewhere, is
a fiction, as the staves are, and the stems,
and the tempi, and the hair.

It's one damn thing
and then another, we've agreed, although
we know it's only one thing with repeats.

II. Andante cantabile

Your hair is map or score or semblable
(it sees us), what if we were wheat I say
perhaps, I say the change becomes us but
at least we're not, so different are the bars
of either cross on which our summer hangs
all tress and sinew; or the white hair now
—yes yes we're only talking—or the white
between the signatures, the dominant
of snow.

We play a different pitch, we try
to keep our feet from turning in this line
we think about extension with, as time's
supposed to have elapsed, the hair a dead
thing growing out of living surfaces—

exhausted yes but undeterred.

                       I say
our substance is replaced by something more
and less ourselves; I say the wheat retains
its shape no matter what the wind consumes.
The hothead strings reprise the melody
the oboe sings before its moment ends,
the *rallentando* deepens on the sound
of two French horns an octave low, which grounds
the harmony.

             Your hair is map or guise,
a soloist of certain form, an old
diversion of the horsehair bow. It asks
if form outlasts its forms, as if the phrase
could comment on its many episodes.

III. Rondeau: Andante grazioso
Not the silence after music but
the sound the earless hear—

                      the notes fly up,
the light glares through their bat-skin heads, their black
stems fluttering.

              Because you're driving I
am not, because it's Tuesday and the map
unfolds to be the same size as the state,
because your hair is now the river or
a rosined bow expecting its relief
of violins, the liquids of the keyed
throat's loosed cadenza pour across the black-
topped road.

            Before we make the highway winds
which were inaudible to any but

the subtlest ear begin to resonate
like hairs along the tympanum. They play
the movement almost perfectly effaced,
in which, by way of being heard, the real's
made real—

        Listen. Now the violins
have posed a dissonance upon a drone,
the way you pose a wrist upon a wrist,
the way the fields come brighter farther on
but colder if there isn't any sleep
before the coda, and the final faint
decisions of the strings are swallowed up
despite the fiercer bowing of your hair.

SOLVING FOR *y*

Everyone is prattling on the train.
It's not the conversations but the rush
of many voices lofted up like smoke
from scattered backyard fires. The neighbors burn

last year's detritus: crappy stripped-off sticks,
some scraps of hemp, discarded copies of
Discover—up and down the Neck. The sea
is swaying, swaying, cursing in the voice

of Paris stamping on the Spartan shore.
Or else it murmurs in the person of
a lover N— (the lover's lover) leaves
in bed to seek engagements someplace else.

Seaweed shimmies in the waves in tight
black tangents. Sparrows dither in the brakes.

Still the rush of voices on the train
is lofted up. Still the sparrows drift
and blunder. Still the moon's a quarter and
the sun's a buck. The stars are out of reach.

At dusk the placket of the sky is rubbed
threadbare, while naked space, suggestively
illumined from behind, disports its limbs.
Why is full disclosure such a bitch?

Why is knowledge partial, if at all?
The sea enjoins on either side. Conceive
of chitchat on the train such intercourse
of heaven, such clatter of the gods. Assert

such clinking of the clunking heart, which thumps
and creaks. Let *x* approach infinity.

NOTES

"Song of Urthona": In William Blake's prophetic books, Urthona is the primordial man, one of four members of Albion. Urthona represents the creative imagination, or the Divine in man. His occupation is blacksmith, his art poetry, his sense hearing, his direction North.

"Arcanum XXII: The Pinioned Man": The named cards of the tarot deck comprise the Major Arcana—from The Fool (0) to The World (XXI). This poem imagines an additional, twenty-second card.

"Wellesley, Massachusetts": Section 1, line 2, alludes to the Ghost in *Hamlet*: "Upon my secure hour thy uncle stole, / With juice of cursed hebenon in a vial, / And in the porches of mine ears did pour / The leprous distilment. . . ." Lines 21 and 22 (slightly mis)quote Ahab's soliloquy in Chapter 132 of *Moby-Dick*. Lines 23 and 24 are words attributed to Jesus at the Passover, referring to "that man by whom the Son of man is betrayed" (Matthew 23: 24).

"Manipura, Out of Tiphereth": Tiphereth ("adornment" in Hebrew) is a position on the Kabbalistic Tree of Life. Manipura ("city of jewels" in Sanskrit) is the third chakra, seated in the belly and associated with the solar plexus.

"Thomas Ball Confronts the Future": Thomas Ball, singer and self-taught sculptor from Charlestown, Massachusetts, created the sculpture of George Washington astride a horse, first unveiled in the Boston Public Garden in 1869.

The sections in "To Xcalak" take their titles from the names of towns along the Costa Maya on Mexico's Caribbean coast.

"Sauve" and "St-Bresson" are the names of towns in the south of France (Gard, Languedoc).

"E-Mail in the Manner of Frank O'Hara" is for Leesteffy Jenkins.

"A Night Out with Isabella de Hainaut": Isabella de Hainaut was Queen of France, born in 1170 AD at Lille. She was crowned at age 10 at St-Denis, and died at age 20 bearing the future Louis VII of France. Her husband, Philip Augustus, waged war against Flanders, from which he had gained the province of Artois as Isabella's dowry. *Semper eadem* ("Always the same") was the motto of Elizabeth I and of her mother, Anne Boleyn.

"The Hair Concerto" takes its section titles from the three movements of Mozart's Violin Concerto No. 4 in D major, K 218.

Author photo by Jennifer Flescher

Jonathan Weinert grew up in Wellesley, Massachusetts. He is a graduate of Brandeis University and the Spalding University MFA in Writing Program. Jonathan serves as web editor for the letterpress literary journal *Tuesday; An Art Project,* as a poetry editor for the online journal *Perihelion,* and as an advisor at the Low-Residency MFA Program in Creative Writing at Lesley University in Cambridge, Massachusetts.

www.jonathanweinert.net

ABOUT NIGHTBOAT BOOKS

Nightboat Books, a nonprofit organization, seeks to develop audiences for writers whose work resists convention and transcends boundaries. We publish books rich with poignancy, intelligence, and risk. Please visit our website, www.nightboat.org, to learn more about us and how you can support our future publications.

NIGHTBOAT TITLES

The Lives of a Spirit/Glasstown: Where Something Got Broken by Fanny Howe

The Truant Lover by Juliet Patterson (Winner of the 2004 Nightboat Poetry Prize)

Radical Love: 5 Novels by Fanny Howe

Glean by Joshua Kryah (Winner of the 2005 Nightboat Poetry Prize)

The Sorrow and the Fast of It by Nathalie Stephens

Envelope of Night: Selected and Uncollected Poems, 1966-1990 by Michael Burkard

FORTHCOMING TITLES

Your Body Figured by Douglas A. Martin

Dura by Myung Mi Kim

Absence Where As by Nathalie Stephens

Our books are available through Small Press Distribution (www.spdbooks.org).

NIGHTBOAT SUPPORTERS

The following individuals have supported the publication of this book. We thank them for their generosity and commitment to the mission of Nightboat Books:

Kazim Ali

Jennifer Chapis

Sarah Heller

David and Marci Rae Johnson

Kathleen and Robert Klein

Christopher and Jill Noon

K. Alma Peterson

Sean C. Safford

Peter R. Waldor

Frank and Lois Weinert

Leslie Williams

In addition, this book has been made possible, in part, by a grant from the New York State Council on the Arts Literature Program.

State of the Arts

NYSCA